Generis

PUBLISHING

Charterer's Risks and Liabilities

Charterer's Risks and Liabilities, Negligence Clause in Charterparty and Protection and Indemnity Insurance

EZGI CAGIRAN

CIP a Camerei Naționale a Cărții

Cagiran, Ezgi.

Charterer's Risks and Liabilities : Charterer's Risks and Liabilities, Negligence Clause in Charterparty and Protection and Indemnity Insurance / Ezgi Cagiran. – Chișinău : Generis Publishing, 2020 (Print on demand). – 41 p.

Referințe bibliogr.: p. 38-39 și în subsol.

ISBN 978-9975-153-62-1.

347.453:656.614.2

C 12

Cover image: www.unsplash.com/photos/CpsTAUPoScw

Generis Publishing
Online orders: www.generis-publishing.com
Orders by email: info@generis-publishing.com

LIST OF ABBREVIATIONS

Cir.	:	Circuit
Co.	:	Company
E.g.	:	For example
Fr.	:	French
Ltd.	:	Limited
No.	:	Number
p.	:	Page
pp.	:	Pages
US	:	The United States
v.	:	Versus
Vol.	:	Volume

I. CHARTERER'S RISKS AND LIABILITIES

a. INTRODUCTION

i. Charterparty

Charterparty is the name of the contract between the charterer and the shipowner for the lease of whole or part of a vessel for one or more voyage or voyages.

ii. Charterer

The party who leases the vessel in this context is called the charterer.

iii. Carrier

In respect of liabilities for loss of or damage to cargo, charterers may, depending on the contract terms and the applicable laws, be considered as the legal "carrier" of the cargo. In such cases the charterer may in the first instance be responsible for risks and liabilities for cargo loss or damage, even though they may have rights of recourse against the shipowner or other third-parties.

b. TYPES OF CHARTERER

i. Demise or Bareboat Charterers

Demise charterparty is the contract by which the shipowner passes the possession and the control of the vessel to the charterer. Demise charterers are in essence leasing the ship without the crew. In terms of risk and liability, the charterer is assuming responsibility for maintaining, manning and operating the ship. Demise charterer needs the same insurance protection through P&I, H&M and ancillary covers as a shipowner.

ii.   Time Charterers

Time charterparty is the contract by which the charterer hires the vessel for a specific period. Time charterers don't have the responsibility for maintenance, repair, manning and navigation of the vessel, but they have the risk and responsibility for the commercial operation of the ship. They make a number of major decisions about the ship. They assume responsibility for matters such as when, where, how and what cargo is loaded, carried and discharged from the vessel. As a result, they assume liabilities for death, injury or damage to property arising from those decisions. They also place their own property such as bunkers, containers and equipment on board the vessel, and so expose them to marine perils.

iii.   Voyage Charterers

Here the shipowner charters the vessel to the charterer for one or more specific voyages. Voyage charterers assume less risk than time charterers because decisions such as when, where and how cargo is loaded are usually a matter of shared responsibility with the shipowner; but voyage charterers often assume responsibility for all or part of loading and discharge operations and for risks associated with the inherent qualities and condition of the cargo.

c. RISING OF RISKS AND LIABILITIES OF CHARTERER

i.   By Contract

Charterers' principal contractual risks arise under the charterparty, cargo booking notes and contracts with stevedores (workers at dock). All these contracts expose charterers to liability for loss of or damage to property (such as cargo or the vessel) and/or personal injury (such as to stevedores or ship's crew).

ii. In Tort or Delict

Typically liability for death or personal injury to third parties such as crewmen or stevedores is caused by the negligence of the charterers or their employees.

iii. Statutory Liability

These are fines, customs penalties, failure to provide safe working systems and oil pollution.

d. COMMON SITUATIONS WHERE A CHARTERER MAY FACE LIABILITY

i. Loss of or Damage to Cargo

This is a charterer's most important area of risk. The charterer faces liability in two distinct ways.

- First, he may be found directly liable to the cargo owner,

- because he issued his own bill of lading, or

- because under the relevant law (which will depend on where the accident occurred, or where the vessel trades, or the bill of lading terms), he may be determined by the courts to be the "carrier" under the Bill of Lading.

- Secondly, he may be liable for damage to cargo because he has to indemnify the shipowner under either a charter contract or a booking note. He typically may have to indemnify owners under the charter for cargo damage caused by bad stowage or defective lashing.

ii.   Personal Injury

Because under many time or voyage charters, the charterer remains responsible in whole or in part for arranging and paying for stevedoring and other loading and discharging operations, he may be held liable for death or injury of any person in those operations, a stevedore or other port worker or a member of the ship's crew.

In many jurisdictions - particularly in the United States – the courts may find charterers wholly responsible for death and personal injury, or they may decide to find both owners and charterers liable to compensate the injured party.

iii.   Pollution

In certain jurisdictions, the operator of the vessel includes the charterer according to oil pollution legislation – particularly in the USA. So direct liability for oil pollution is a real risk for a charterer.

Time charterers may find themselves liable for pollution, including fines, during bunkering operations. The most serious pollution risk for a charterer probably arises from charterer's orders for the vessel to proceed to an unsafe port, where she sustains a casualty and spills bunkers or cargo. In one case, following the grounding of a tanker in Spain in 1992, the owner's indemnity claim against the charterer in respect of pollution by ship's cargo amounted to some US$65M.

iv.   Damage to Hull

Charterer's liability for loss of or damage to the vessel can range from relatively small claims for routine damage caused by stevedores, to the total loss of the ship. As with serious claims for oil pollution, a charterer may be liable to indemnify the owner for the total loss of the ship as a result of ordering the vessel to an unsafe port. An equally serious risk for any charterer, is loss of or serious damage to the vessel and all or part of its cargo, caused by the dangerous properties of the cargo loaded by the charterer. Fire or explosion of cargoes loaded in containers is an example. The charterer may find himself liable to indemnify the owner for having shipped a dangerous cargo, and then unable to enforce rights of recourse against a shipper. Another ex. is damage to the chartered vessel's machinery by a charterer because of defective bunkers.

v.   Fines

Charterers may also have to pay fines. Fines may also form part of indemnity claims by shipowners against the charterer.

vi.   General Average, Salvage and Special Charges

A time charterer will offer to put his own property on board a vessel in the form of bunkers, containers not carried as cargo and other equipment such as lashing material. So he faces the risk of having to pay general average or salvage costs and special charges in respect of such property on board a vessel which suffers a casualty.

vii.   Legal Costs and Related Expenses

Even where a charterer may finally be able to avoid liability for these risks, he may be exposed to some legal costs and other expenses in defending himself against claims. In the case of a major casualty involving death or serious personal injury, serious damage to cargo, pollution or loss of or serious damage to the vessel, such legal and related costs could be considerable.

Charterers often find themselves engaged in more contractual relationships in the trading of the vessel than a shipowner. There will be at least one charterparty, and maybe two if the vessel is sub-chartered. There will be stevedoring contracts, booking notes, bills of lading and so forth. The greater number of contracts, the greater the potential for disputes between the charterer and his contract partner. Dispute resolution by litigation or otherwise can involve substantial costs.

e. CONCLUSION

The liability environment in which the shipping industry operates is becoming increasingly hostile. The industry is becoming ever more regulated, particularly in areas of safety and pollution. Penalties and costs imposed in respect of pollution and environmental damage have increased worldwide, not only in the USA. Compensation levels for death and injury have also increased. Liability regimes for sea carriers have become more rigorous and the opportunities for ship operators – particularly charterers – to limit their liabilities under the applicable laws have reduced. In certain circumstances, these risks and liabilities are large enough to undermine or destroy the financial base of even the most well-established charterer; that is why an increasing number of charterers recognize the need to take out insurance protection.

II. NEGLIGENCE CLAUSE IN CHARTERPARTY

a. INTRODUCTION

i. General

For more than a century, clauses in bills of lading [1] relieving shipowners or carriers from liability for negligence have been the subject of a spectacular conflict. These types of clauses are called *"negligence clauses"* and are included in *"charterparty"* [2], which is an important instrument of the maritime law. In other words, negligence clauses are the clauses which exclude shipowners' or carriers' liability for all events including their own negligence.

A person who suffers loss or damage at the hand of another, whether in delict (tort) or in contract, may generally invoke the power of the law to claim damages designed to redress the wrong. This redress is not without limits. Even the most expansive system of law requires the loss or damage to be caused by the actions of the defendant. In maritime law, however, the law draws a somewhat different line short of this already limited recompense by allowing a shipowner in appropriate circumstances to limit its liability. The concept of limitation is well-known throughout maritime law and has, in modern times, become a basic premise upon which maritime commerce is conducted. [3]

The transport of the goods by sea is the way of transport, which is used very often. The marine transport has some individual characteristics such as the difficulty of carrying the goods on board. If it is compared to the land transport, it is obvious that the loss of a vessel is much larger than the loss of a track. Nevertheless, the transport by sea is quite important in international carriage of goods. Within this international system of the

---

[1] Bill of lading is a legal instrument, which is issued unilaterally by the carrier, the master or an authorized agency (on behalf of the carrier), comprising the admission of the burden having been delivered to be carried and (after the carriage) the obligation as per which it would be delivered to the holder, who seems beneficiary, at the port of destination in return for the bill.

[2] Fr.: *"charte-partie"*.

[3] John HARE, **Limitation of Liability in Shipping**, University of Cape Town, Nigeria, 2004, p. 2.

marine transport, the carrier, the person, who is obliged to take the cargo from one place to another by sea, and the shipowner, the person, who equips and exploits the vessel, are the most important characters.

The purpose of this dissertation is to examine all aspects of the negligence clauses under the charterparty; with the historical background and legal issues regarding these types of clauses. The method used herein is a combination of historical and legal approach with regard to the negligence clauses in the light of the *limitation of liability* concept, which is the basis of such clauses.

As the negligence clause in the charterparty is a quite particular issue of the maritime law, the general information concerning the contract of affreightment and the charterparty is given in order to clarify the technical terms related to the maritime law before entering into details. The different types of the charterparty, which are the voyage charterparty, time charterparty and the demise charterparty shall also be defined under this party. After this brief information within the first chapter dedicated to the introduction, the evolution of the negligence clauses in the light of the limitation of liability concept will be introduced in the second chapter, where the historical background of the limitation of liability concept and the place of such clauses on the international scene will be studied. The third chapter shall concentrate on the negligence clause on the basis of the five basic questions for the review of the contract clauses, which are "who", "to whom", "what", "when" and "where". The forth chapter shall focus on the legal basis of the negligence clauses by virtue of related international treaties. These essential international treaties are the Hague Rules, the Hague-Visby Rules and the Hamburg Rules. Finally, under the fifth chapter, the question of the validity of the negligence clauses shall be introduced with regard to different system such as the British and the American systems.

iv.   Contract of affreightment [4] and charterparty

1. Contract of affreightment

Cargo vessels are usually under contracts by which the shipowner, in return for a sum of money – the freight – agrees to carry goods by sea, or to furnish the services of a vessel for the purpose of such carriage. Such contracts, commonly called contracts of affreightment, encompass a heterogeneous mass of maritime agreements, comprising such differing types as contracts for the lease of a vessel (bare boat or demise charters), voyage and time charterparties, and bills of lading . [5] Briefly, the contract of affreightment is a generic term used in respect of all contracts of carriage of goods by sea.

2. Charterparty

The contract between the charterer (one who charters the ship) and the shipowner is known as a "*charterparty*".[6] Generally, it is considered the use of the ship by the owner, in carrying his own goods, or those of others, under bills of lading only. He may, however, prefer to let his ship out to others, for their use. This is commonly done by a *charterparty*; an instrument of frequent use and great importance among merchants. No especial form is necessary, and it is quite common to introduce into it any stipulations or provisions which the peculiar character of the voyage, or the purposes of the parties may require. [7] A charterparty of affreightment, therefore, is a contract in writing, for the letting to freight of the whole or part of a ship, for one or more voyage or voyages. [8]

---

[4] Fr.: "*contrat d'affrètement*".

[5] Martin DOCKRAY, **Cases & Materials on the Carriage of Goods by Sea**, Cavendish Publishing, Third Edition, 2004, p. 2.

[6] Indira CARR - Peter STONE, **International Trade Law**, Routledge, Oxon, 2014, p. 154.

[7] Theophilus PARSONS, **A Treatise on Maritime Law, including the Law of Shipping; the Law of Marine Insurance; and the Law and Practice of Admiralty**, Little Brown and Company, Boston, 1859, p. 229.

[8] Edward LAWES, **A Practical Treatise on Charter parties of Affreightment, Bills of Lading, and Stoppage in Transitu, With an Appendix of Precedents**, Printed by S. Brooke, 35, Paternoster-

It is mentioned hereinabove that there is no requirement for the charterparty to be made in written form. However, it is usual for the charterparty to be in writing in practice. The charterparty will identify the vessel, the cargo it is to carry, the voyage(s) or time for which the ship is made available and contains terms in respect of the various responsibilities and liabilities of the shipowner and the charterer. [9]

In practice, the parties will variably select a standard form of charterparty as the basis of their agreement, to which they will probably attach additional clauses to suit their own requirements. These standard forms have a variety of origins. A considerable number which have appeared during the past century, however, are the products of the documentary committees of such bodies as the United Kingdom Chamber of Shipping, the Baltic and International Maritime Conference and the Japanese Shipping Exchange, on many of which both shipowner and charterer interests are represented. The existence of these standard forms is of considerable advantage in international trade where the parties may be domiciled in different countries and their negotiations hampered by language problems. [10]

The charterparties are classified into three basic types as the voyage charterparties, the time charterparties and the demise charterparties.

a. Voyage charterparty [11]

Under the voyage charterparty, the shipowner agrees to charter the vessel to the charterer for one or more specified voyages. The owner of the vessel agrees to carry the cargo from one port to another on a particular voyage or voyages. [12] The vessel remains

---

Row and Sold by Messrs. Butterworth and Son, Fleet Street; Clarke and Sons, Portugal Street; R. Pheney, Inner Temple Lane; and S. Sweet, Chancery Lane, London, 1813, p. 2.

[9] Indira CARR - Peter STONE, op.cit, 2014, p. 154.

[10] John F. WILSON, **Carriage of Goods by Sea**, Pearson - Longman, Sixth Edition, Southampton, 2008, p. 1.

[11] Fr.: *"contrat d'affrètement au voyage"*.

[12] Robert FORCE, **Admiralty and Maritime Law**, Federal Judicial Center 2004, p. 42.

under the control of the shipowner, who is responsible for equipping and manning the vessel. The shipowner, in a voyage charterparty, undertakes to transport the goods to the port(s) specified in the charterparty. [13]

b. Time charterparty [14]

Under a time charterparty, the charterer hires the vessel for a specified period of time. As in a voyage charterparty, the shipowner retains the control of the ship and the employees on board the ship. However, the charterer is responsible for its deployment, the number of voyages it undertakes and the destination of the voyages. The shipowner, in a time charterparty, does not undertake to transport the goods to a specified port(s) as in a voyage charterparty. [15] In other words, the time charterparty is a contract for the hire of a named vessel for a specified period of time, during which the charterer may use the vessel as he wishes with certain exceptions. The time during which the vessel is chartered differs from contract to contract and can amount to several months or years or only amount to the time that is necessary to undertake one complete voyage.

c. Demise charterparty [16]

Also known as a bareboat charterparty, in a demise charterparty, the shipowner passes the possession and the control of the ship to the charterer. The shipowner is no longer responsible for equipping the ship or employing the crew as in a voyage or time charterparty. For the duration of the charter, the charterer is responsible for manning, equipping and insuring it. [17] By this type of charter, the shipowner leases his entire vessel and the charterer has the responsibility of operating it as though it were his own vessel. [18]

---

[13] Indira CARR - Peter STONE, op.cit., 2014, p. 155.

[14] Fr.: *"contrat d'affrètement à temps"*.

[15] India CARR - Peter STONE, op.cit., 2014, p. 155.

[16] Fr.: *"contrat d'affrètement coque-nue"*.

[17] Indira CARR – Peter STONE, op.cit., 2014, p. 156.

[18] The difference between the bare boat charterparty and the other types of charterparty is to be found in the judgment of **Sea & Land Securities Ltd v. William Dickinson & Co Ltd** [1942] 2 KB 65 at

As the name implies, the bare vessel is chartered. The shipowner, for the period covered by the charterparty, loses control of his vessel. Having complete control, the bareboat charterer also has the rather heavy responsibilities of an owner. [19]

b. EVOLUTION OF NEGLIGENCE CLAUSES IN LIGHT OF "LIMITATION OF LIABILITY" CONCEPT

i.   Historical background

The limitation of liability is a concept which is widespread in the law relating to the transportation of goods. It is a common practice for all types of transport. Regarding the transport by sea, the basic principle of shipowners' or carriers' limitation of liability is that the shipowner or the carrier is liable but this liability can be reduced under certain circumstances. It should be underlined that the shipowner or the carrier may claim a limit upon their damages with respect to liability arising from collision, allusion, grounding, cargo damage, death or personal injuries. As one of the basic rules of law is the liability of the wrongdoer, the limitation of liability may be considered as a privilege for shipowners or carriers.

The notion of the limitation of liability in maritime law is of uncertain origin, although it may possibly be linked to the Roman law notion of *noxae deditio* in terms of which an owner could discharge liability for damage to another individual by giving up the offending instrument. [20]

---

p. 69: *"The distinction between the demise and other forms of charter contract is as clear as the difference between the agreement a man makes when he hires a boat in which to row himself and the contract he makes with a boatman to take him for a row."*

[19] Roman T. KEENAN, "Charter Parties and Bills of Lading", **Marquette Law Review**, Vol. 42, Milwaukee, 1959, p. 347.

[20] Gotthard GAUCI, "Limitation of Liability in Maritime Law, an anachronism?", **Marine Policy**, Vol. 19, No. 1, 1995, p. 65.

The bills of lading, as defined hereinabove, is a legal instrument playing an important role in international sale transactions. Terms contained in the bills of lading play a central part in determining the rights and liabilities of the parties to the contract. Most bills of lading issued today are subject to international conventions – the Hague Rules, the Hague-Visby Rules and the Hamburg Rules, which impose on the carrier minimum responsibilities and liabilities that cannot be lessened with suitable clauses in the contract. The current legal regime relating to bills of lading, however, is a consequence of developments that started approximately 200 years ago. [21]

ii.   Place of negligence clauses on the international scene

1. Different systems

At common law, the carrier was strictly liable for the safe transport of the cargo to its destination and delivery to the designated person.[22] The carrier could however disclaim this strict liability by inserting suitable clauses in the contract of carriage. The increase in the ocean traffic in the 19th century increased the use of exemption clauses. In the context of contracts of carriage of goods by sea, the shipowner, the stronger of the contracting parties, inevitably inserted all embracing exclusion clauses. Carriers were exempted from liability for loss or damage from perils of the sea, decay, strikes, deviation to unseaworthy ships and their own negligence. The exclusion clauses operated totally in the carrier's favour and the goods were carried entirely at the merchant's risk. Judges in Britain (…) were sympathetic to such clauses. And of course, Britain, a nation with huge maritime interests, had a lot to gain with the increase in the volume of ocean traffic. [23]

---

[21] Indira CARR – Peter STONE, **International Trade Law**, Routledge – Cavendish, Fourth Edition, Oxon, 2010, p. 229.

[22] In the case of **Boucher v. Lawson** in 1733, the shipowner was found personally liable for the loss of cargo of gold bullion stolen by the master. The rationale limitation of liability in this period was to protect the innocent owner from unlimited liability for negligence of those particular servants who were beyond his physical control. The aim was protecting shipowners from unlimited liability in case of negligence of people working beyond their control. As a result of the case, the Responsibilities of Shipowners Act was made in 1733. (Cas. T. hard 53; 95 E. R. 116)

[23] Indira CARR – Peter STONE, op.cit., 2010, p. 229.

The liberal British attitude to disclaimers in bills of lading was not followed in other jurisdictions. The US Supreme Court, for instance, read exclusion clauses extremely restrictively. [24] The United States enacted the Harter Act in 1893 in order to limit the shipowners' freedom of contract and protect the cargo owner [25].

2. Towards a unified system

The United States, having first succeeded in reaching a compromise between the conflicting interests of carriers and shippers in its domestic law, took the lead in urging a uniform international regulation of the carriers' liability. The need for such regulation was generally felt, and action was taken by interested business groups and international institutions. After several decades of preparatory work, the movement for uniformity culminated in an international convention "for the unification of certain rules of law relating to bills of lading", signed in Brussels, on August 25, 1924. [26]

The International Convention for the Unification of Certain Rules of Bills of Lading [27], providing for a minimum level of liability for the carriers, was signed by major trading nations [28]. The 1924 Brussels Convention on the Bills of Lading, more commonly known as the Hague Rules, has been one of the most widely accepted of all the maritime conventions. [29] Most of maritime nations, including the United States, have ratified or adhered to the Brussels Convention; others without adhering, have

---

[24] Ibid, p. 230.

[25] The Harter Act shall be detailed hereinafter under the Section V.

[26] Athanassios N. YIANNOPOULOS, "Conflict Problems in International Bills of Lading: Validity of Negligence Clauses", **Louisiana Law Review**, Vol. 18, No. 4, June 1958, p. 610.

[27] This Convention is most commonly known as the *"Hague Rules"* because the work on them commenced at a meeting of the International Law Association at the Hague in the Netherlands in 1921.

[28] The United Kingdom implemented the Hague Rules with the Carriage of Goods by Sea Act in 1924. Canada is also one of the parties of the Hague Rules. As this is the first try to the unification of certain rules related to the bills of lading, most of the European countries will take place later, in the Hague-Visby Rules. France, for instance, ratified the Hague Rules with the law of Avril 9th, 1936.

[29] Upendra BAXI, "Unification of Private Maritime International Law through Treaties – An Assessment", **Indian Year Book of International Affairs**, 1965, p. 128.

enacted domestic regulation incorporating the rules agreed upon in Brussels. However, this substantial uniformity of domestic legislation has not eliminated the conflicts problems arising in the determination of validity of negligence clauses [30] inserted in bills of lading involving international contracts. [31]

Failings of the Hague Rules however surfaced over time as a consequence of litigation and developments in shipping technology. For instance, the defences and limitation of liability afforded by the Rules did not extend to the servants or agents of the carriers. [32] This led to the drafting of the Brussels Protocol, which revised the Hague Rules in 1968. This protocol, called Hague-Visby Rules, was not adopted by all the signatories to the Hague Rules [33].

c. NEGLIGENCE CLAUSES IN FIVE STEPS

As it was presented hereinabove, the negligence clause is the clause in a bill of lading or charterparty, which seeks to relieve the shipowner or the carrier of liability for losses and damages caused by the negligence of his servants or agents. In order to simplify the issue of negligence clauses, such clauses will be analyzed hereinafter on the basis of certain key questions.

i.   Who

Under negligence clauses, the shipowner or the carrier shall not be liable for loss or damage to the goods as a result of the neglect of the master, mariner, pilot or the servants of the shipowner or the carrier in the navigation or management of this ship.

---

[30] The issue of the validity of the negligence clauses shall be discussed hereinafter under the Section V.

[31] Athanassios YIANNOPOULAS, op.cit., p. 610.

[32] Indira CARR – Peter STONE, op.cit., 2010, p. 230.

[33] The US, for instance, is not a party whereas most of the European countries became party to the Hague-Visby Rules.

Within the scope of negligence clauses, the persons exempted from liability are the shipowner or the carrier. [34] One point, which creates confusion in this context, is that, regarding the person who is protected under the negligence clauses, the term used within the doctrine, may vary. The terms *shipowner* or *carrier* may be used by authors. The use of both terms together is also a way to refer to the persons to be protected under negligence clauses. In order to make this confusion clear, the international conventions on maritime issues including the liabilities of the parties to affreightment contracts is reviewed. It is in evidence that, in these conventions, the term *carrier* is used as an umbrella term. As per the Hague Rules and Hague-Visby Rules, the carrier is the owner or charterer who enters into contract of carriage with a shipper. [35] According to the Hamburg Rules, the carrier is any person by whom or in whose name a contract of carriage has been concluded with a shipper so this term covers the actual and contractual carrier. [36] Consequently, the term *carrier* is a term covering both the *carrier* and the *shipowner* in the scope of negligence clauses.

ii.   To whom

Under the negligence clauses, the shipowner or the carrier is exempted from liability for negligence towards the cargo owner. The person who enters into a contractual relationship with the shipowner or the carrier, in order to make the cargo carried between the determined ports, is the cargo owner. The protection under the negligence clause is for the losses or the damages to the goods, which are going to be carried or being carried, so the carrier or the shipowner is exempted from this liability vis-à-vis the owner of the goods.

---

[34] In the case **Mississippi Shipping Co. v. Zander and Company**, the vessel collided with a pier while departing; the cargo was exposed to sea water, and was damaged. After resolving that the voyage had commenced, overriding the allegation of unseaworthiness, the fifth circuit of United States Court of Appeal held the negligence resulting in collision and subsequent cargo damage to be an act of navigation and a carrier avoided liability. (270 F.2d 345, 5th Cir. 1959)

[35] Article 1 (a) of the Hague Rules and of the Hague-Visby Rules.

[36] Article 1.1, 10 and 11 of the Hamburg Rules.

es, as stated hereinabove, are the clauses, with the purpose of he shipowner from the liability for *negligence* of agents in the ιanagement of the vessel. The negligence herein covers the ng, stowage, custody, care, or proper delivery of cargo, or the negligence in ... g, manning, provisioning, outfitting, or otherwise making the vessel seaworthy.

Under a voyage charterparty, the vessel is manned and navigated by the owner's crew. To the extent that a voyage charterer obtains only the carrying capacity of a particular vessel, the charterer is not responsible for maintenance, repairs to the vessel, or injuries to third parties arising from the crew's operational negligence. [37] As with a voyage charterparty, the vessel owner under a time charter is responsible for the navigation and management of the vessel, subject to conditions set out in the charterparty. [38] Because the time charterer obtains only the carrying capacity of a particular vessel, the charterer is not responsible for maintenance, repairs to the vessel, or injuries to third parties arising from the crew's operational negligence. [39] In a demise charterparty, the charterer not only leases the carrying capacity of the vessel but, unlike a time or voyage charter, also obtains a degree of control over the management and navigation of the vessel. Because a demise charter transfers the possession and control of the vessel to the charterer, one who takes a vessel on demise is responsible for maintenance, repairs, or damages caused to third parties by the crew's negligent navigation of the vessel. Thus, the owner who has demised its vessel will generally not be liable *in personam* for the fault or negligence by the crew, the charterer will be primarily liable. [40]

iv. When

As stated hereinabove, the exemption from the liability for negligence of the shipowner or the carrier is only accepted for the neglect in the navigation or

---

[37] Robert FORCE, op.cit., p. 42.

[38] Ibid.

[39] Ibid, p. 43.

[40] Ibid.

management of the ship. This means that the neglect out of
management of the vessel is not covered under the negligence clauses.
the period for these clauses to run, is limited to the navigation and the man
the vessel. The exemption from liability of the shipowner or the carrier, in
neglect of the mentioned persons, is not covered under the negligence clauses it
mentioned negligent acts occur out of the navigation and the management of the vessel.

v.   Where

The shipowner or the carrier is exempted from liability for the losses or damages to
the cargo by the negligence clauses and the negligence in question is limited to the
issue of the navigation and the management of the vessel. It may be concluded that the
situations, which may lead to the exemption of liability of the shipowner or the carrier
under negligence clauses, are encountered only at the places where the cargo is situated
and damaged.

As stated hereinabove under the subsection (c), the negligence covers the negligence
in the loading, stowage, custody, care, or proper delivery of cargo, or the negligence in
equipping, manning, provisioning, outfitting, or otherwise making the vessel
seaworthy. This means that the negligence clauses may be discussed for the negligent
acts in port for certain limited acts such as loading or on board for all the other acts.

d. NEGLIGENCE CLAUSES REGULATIONS

i.   Hague Rules

As per the article 4/2 of the Hague Rules;

*"Neither the carrier nor the ship shall be responsible for loss or damage arising or
resulting from (a) act, neglect, or default of the master, mariner, pilot, or the servants
of the carrier in the navigation or in the management of the ship (…).".*

The article 4/3 of the Hague Rules is as the following;

"The shipper shall not be responsible for loss or damage sustained by the carrier or the ship arising or resulting from any cause without the act, fault or neglect of the shipper, his agents or his servants.".

The two limbs of this exception – fault in navigation and fault in management – have been difficult to interpret. Fault in the navigation of the ship has been construed as applying to situations where, due to the negligent act on the part of the master or crew, the vessel has been grounded or has collided with another vessel. [41]

ii.   Hague-Visby Rules

The Hague-Visby Rules [42] do not differ from the Hague Rules concerning the negligence clauses. Identically, the carrier and the ship are not responsible for the loss or the damage arising or resulting from the neglect of the master, the mariner, the pilot, or the servants of the carrier only if the neglect is related to the navigation or the management of the vessel.

iii.   Hamburg Rules

The Hamburg Rules are the rules resulting from the United Nations International Convention on the Carriage of Goods by Sea and are adopted in Hamburg on March 31st, 1978. [43] The goal of the Hamburg Rules was to reach a uniform legal base for the

---

[41] Indira CARR – Peter STONE, op.cit., 2010, p. 247.

[42] The United Kingdom and most of the European countries including France are parties of The Hague-Visby Rules whereas the United States is not a party to this Convention.

[43] Certain countries signed the Hamburg Rules but did not ratify. E.g. France and United States signed the Hamburg Rules in 1979, but they have not ratified yet. England is not even a signatory. For the list of the participant countries, see :

https://treaties.un.org/pages/ViewDetails.aspx?src=TREATY&mtdsg_no=XI-D-3&chapter=11&lang=en

transportation of the goods on oceangoing vessels and to eliminate the defects of the Hague Rules. At this point, the question concerning the negligence clauses was why the shipowner was not liable for negligence in management and navigation. The view would be that this is an old-fashioned exception dating back to sailing vessels and says when maritime ventures were hazardous. One can now establish what shipowners ought to have done in particular circumstances; why can they not be liable for negligence in navigation and management? [44] That is why the carrier must prove he, his servants or agents, took all measures that could reasonably be required to avoid the occurrence and its consequences.

The basic rule is that the carrier is liable in certain circumstances defined unless he proves that he, his servants or agents took all measures that could reasonably be required to avoid the occurrence and its consequences.[45] The Article 5.1 of the Hamburg Rules is stipulated as follows;

"The Carrier is liable for loss resulting from loss of or damage to the goods as well as from delay in delivery, if the occurrence which caused the loss, damage or delay took place while the goods were in his charge as defined in Article 4, unless the carrier proves that he, his servants or agents took all measures that could reasonably be required to avoid the occurrence and its consequences."

e. VALIDITY OF NEGLIGENCE CLAUSES

The conflict regarding the validity of the negligence clauses in maritime law is an issue, which was commenced to be discussed long time ago. In countries where cargo interests dominated, "negligence" clauses were declared invalid; in other countries, where hull interests prevailed, such clauses were given effect under the cover of an almost unlimited freedom of contracting. By the end of the 19th century, the world was

---

[44] Francis REYNOLDS, The Hague Rules, the Hague-Visby Rules, and the Hamburg Rules, **the MLAANZ New Wealand Branch Conference**, Tokaanu, 1990, p. 28.

[45] Francis REYNALDS, op.cit., p. 30.

divided into shippers' countries and carriers' countries [46]; and the domestic policy was frequently carried into the international field by the adoption of conflicts rules safeguarding the application of domestic standards to bills of lading international contracts. Thus, due varying domestic standards and conflicts rules, the same clause inserted into an international bill of lading could be valid in one country and invalid in another. [47]

As it was presented hereinabove, the substantial uniformity of domestic regulation in the Hague Rules did not eliminate the problems of validity of negligence clauses especially which were inserted into bills of lading of international contracts. The area of the application of the (uniform) forum law, as well as choice of law rules, differ from country to country; and depending on the place of litigation, the same bill of lading may or may not be subject to the Brussels Convention even where the forum is in a signatory country and the contract of affreightment involves contacts with another signatory country. It seems therefore that, as in the past, a negligence clause may be given effect in one country and denied effect in another, contrary to both the letter and spirit of the Brussels Convention. [48]

i.   England

In certain areas, especially the North Atlantic, at least some shipowners were apparently excluding virtually all, or at any rate a great deal of, their liability. Now, what they call the negligence clause which, in effect, excluded all shipowners' liability for all events including their own negligence, was valid in England before English courts, subject to presumptions that the basic liability of the shipowner in regard to seaworthiness and care of cargo was not excluded unless clearly stated. But this clause in most forms was clear and therefore was valid. [49] In England, the rule of freedom of

---

[46] E.g., England and France were predominantly "carrier-countries", while the United States was a shipper's country.

[47] Athanassios N. YIANNOPOULOS, op.cit., p. 609.

[48] Ibid, p. 611.

[49] Francis REYNOLDS, op.cit., p. 17.

contract applied whereby carriers were permitted to contractually opt out of liability even when it was fault based. [50]

ii.   United States

The courts in the United States refused to enforce clauses that purported to exempt a carrier from liability based on its negligence. [51] In the United States, such a clause was not always valid. It might be held invalid as contrary to public policy. [52] As per the United States law, the contract of affreightment was generally enforceable according to its own terms. Since the 1880s, however, the American federal courts resolutely refused to enforce "unreasonable" conditions inserted into bills of lading, such as clauses which exempted the shipowner from liability for his own or his servants' negligence.

Contracts of affreightment involving significant foreign contracts were governed by the law selected by the parties, and in the absence of agreement, by the law of the place of contracting as impliedly intended. Nevertheless, unreasonable limitations of liability contained in contracts which were to be performed in part or in whole in the United States, were considered contrary to the public policy of the forum and of no effect, whether the American of foreign law governed. [53]

As this legal system could not safeguard the interests of American shippers, the growth of the American shipping industry was not encouraged, that is why the Harter Act was passed in 1893.

---

[50] Robert FORCE, op.cit., p. 53.

[51] Ibid, p. 53.

[52] Francis REYNOLDS, op.cit., p.17.

[53] Athanassios N. YIANNOPOULOS, op.cit., p. 613.

1. Harter Act

Under the Harter Act, in 1893, clauses relieving the shipowner from liability for loss and damage to the cargo arising from negligence were declared "null and void and of no effect"; but the shipowner was relieved from liability for negligence "in navigation or in the management" of the vessel, if he used due diligence to make his vessel seaworthy. Initially designed to apply to foreign trade only, the Harter Act was extended to cover domestic trade as well, and was declared applicable to all shipments to and from the ports of the United States. This act, still in force insofar as not superseded by the Carriage of Goods by Sea Act, 1936, plays an important role in the regulation of both the domestic and the international trade of the United States. [54]

2. Carriage of Goods by Sea Act

The Carriage of Goods by Sea Act was enacted in 1936 in view of the pending ratification by the United States of the Brussels Convention of 1924. According to this Act, clauses relieving the carrier from liability for negligence in the loading, handling, stowing, carrying, keeping, and in the discharge of the goods are declared null and void; the carrier, however, is relieved from liability arising from negligence in the "navigation or management" of the vessel. [55]

İn addition to passing this act, the United States deposited its ratification of the Hague Rules on June 29, 1937. [56]

3. Hague Rules

It's well settled in the United States that all bills of lading covering carriage of hull cargo (other than live animals) to or from the ports of the United States in foreign trade, from the time of loading until discharge, are subject to the Brussels Convention as

---

[54] Ibid, p. 613.

[55] Athanassios N. YIANNOPOULOS, op.cit., p. 615.

[56] Ibid.

incorporated into the Carriage of Goods by Sea Act. [57] Any clause inserted into such bills of lading exonerating the carrier or the ship from liability for negligence (other than in the navigation or management of the vessel), or lessening that liability otherwise than as provided in the Carriage of Goods by Sea Act, is null and void. However, apart from agreements directly exonerating the carrier from liability for negligence, exoneration may be attempted by clauses stipulating the application of a more favorable foreign law or by clauses granting exclusive jurisdiction to the courts of a foreign country. [58] The validity of negligence clauses inserted into this category of contracts will primarily depend on the law selected by the parties. [59] In absence of stipulation as to the applicable law, the liability of the carrier, and the validity of exoneration clauses, will be determined according to the law of the place of contracting, or that of performance, as impliedly intended. [60]

iii.   France

France was one of the countries which juridically accept negligence clauses for a long period of time. In that period, the discussion was about the limit between two notions which are the freedom of contract and the interests of merchandises. These discussions resulted with multiple bills of law in order to limit the freedom of having, in maritime contracts, clauses concerning the exoneration of negligent acts of the master and the crew and also to prohibit negligence clauses. However, the legislator and the judges in France supported the existence of such clauses. The basis of their argument was the freedom of contract.

Following the discussions, the negligence clause is accepted to be valid in France, unless the debtor commits a gross or intentional fault.

---

[57] Ibid, p. 617.

[58] Ibid, p. 618.

[59] Ibid, p. 624.

[60] Ibid, p. 625.

f. CONCLUSION

Throughout the past centuries, the clauses, which aim to exempt the shipowner or the carrier from the liability regarding the loss or the damage to the goods for the negligent acts of their agents, were one of the clauses which were mostly discussed. In the past, the sea was not known as well as it is known today because of the non-existence of the technology. And also, the loss and the damage in the marine transport were huge. The idea concerning the question of the limitation of liability was to protect the shipowner or the carrier from unlimited liability for negligence of agents, who were beyond his physical control. For these essential reasons, the logic of the negligence clauses was, at the beginning, to encourage the shipowners and the carriers to enter into contractual relations with the cargo owners in order to carry their goods. However, due to the technological developments and the developments in the international maritime law, especially concerning the insurance of the vessels, it may be concluded that there is not that much need to these clauses as in the past. Nevertheless, the parties to the contracts of carriage by sea may validly put the clauses exempting the shipowner or the carrier from the liability for the loss or the damage to the goods for the negligent acts of their agents, into their contracts in terms of the freedom of contract. Personally, after examining such clauses in many countries, I think that the best legislation system is the system which allows these clauses to be put in the contracts by the parties on the basis of the freedom of the contract but with certain limitations such as non-existence of gross or intentional fault of the master or his servants. In the contrary case, the fact of prohibiting such clauses would cause the shipowners and the carriers to refrain from entering into such commercial relations because of the gross risks of sea. For this reason, the best way to cope with this issue is to allow negligence clauses under the control of restrictive legislative regulations.

III.   PROTECTION AND INDEMNITY INSURANCE

a. INTRODUCTION

i.   Key Notions

1. Protection and Indemnity Insurance and Clubs

Protection and Indemnity Insurance is one of the three important marine insurance. The other insurances are hull and machinery insurance and cargo insurance. In basic terms, Protection and Indemnity Insurance, commonly known as P&I Insurance, is a ship-owner's insurance which covers legal liabilities to third parties. "Third parties" are any person apart from the ship-owner himself, who may have a legal or contractual claim against the vessel. P&I Insurance is provided by a P&I Club.

A P&I club is a non-governmental, non-profitable mutual (or cooperative) association of marine insurance providers to its members consisting of ship- owners, operators, charterers and seafarers under the member companies.

2. "Protection" and "Indemnity"

The word "Protection" simply means that the insurance covers assistance when a vessel is involved in an accident and the ship-owner and his Master need help. Often the Club's early intervention and assistance will help to head off problems and serve to protect the ship-owner from inflated claims.

P&I Insurance is an indemnity type of insurance, which means that the ship-owner (or member of the club) must demonstrate his loss before the club will pay out (or indemnify him) under the terms of the insurance policy. It is important to bear in mind that the Club never assumes the owner's liability; therefore technically the owner (or member) is always responsible for payments. In practice, the Club takes over the business of handling claims and ensuring that payments are correctly made.

## ii.	History

The concept of protection against maritime perils is a concept coming from the romans in 235 BC. The origin of the protection and indemnity insurance is quite later, in 1836. This is the date of the "Case Vaux v. Salvador", in which two vessels came into collision where. In this case, the collision liability was so big that the insurers could not cover. Afterwards, ship-owners found themselves with liabilities which their traditional hull underwriters were unable or unwilling to cover. In order to solve the problem, groups of ship-owners formed themselves into mutual associations and agreed to share each other's claims. The first P&I Club is created in the UK in 1855, it is now called "Britannia".

These early organizations have now developed into Thirteen P&I Clubs, which are mainly situated in the UK but also in the USA, Japan, Sweden and Norway and which are members of the International Group of P&I Clubs and more than 90% of the world's oceangoing tonnage is insured by them.

b. ROLE OF P&I CLUBS

### i.	Service

The P&I Clubs all operate on a mutual or non-profit basis aiming to call up only sufficient money in each year to meet costs, expenses and claims for that year. There are no shareholders and the members of the P&I Club insure each other.

A P&I Club operates as a mixture of an insurance company, a law firm and a loss adjuster because they should be able to assist a ship-owner in dealing with every aspect of a casualty from finding experts and contractors to deal with the immediate casualty through to legal advice and paying claims.

The P&I Club exists to help the ship-owner and pay his liability claims. Almost always the ship-owner and his Club will work together to solve the problems and it is very rare that a Club will be in dispute with a ship-owner over cover.

The Clubs are unique organisations in that they provide not only insurance cover, but also claims handling (legal) advice and a casualty response service. In managing a ship-owner's liabilities, a Club may have to deal with the loss of two bags of rice or the total loss of a fully loaded vessel. The Club's reaction therefore needs to be highly flexible.

ii.   Cover

P&I Clubs provide cover for a ship-owner's liabilities, not the fabric of the vessel itself. The risks covered will usually include;

- Death and personal injury
- Seamen
- Passengers
- Third parties
- Liabilities in respect of stowaways or persons saved at sea
- Liabilities arising from collisions
- Liabilities arising from groundings
- Liabilities arising from damage to fixed and floating objects
- Liabilities arising from pollution
- Liabilities arising from wreck removal
- Liabilities arising from towage operations
- Liability to cargo together with other legal and other costs associated with dealing these claims.

There are also claims that are not covered by P&I insurance. One of the main reasons is that the club thinks it shall be covered by another insurance that the owner should have taken out. That usually means hull insurance for example. Another reason is that the owner had not taken certain steps to have limited his liability to protect the Club. Today the owners have to comply with legal requirements of the flag state concerning marine safety and environmental protection. Another reason is related to liabilities arising out of the misdelivery of cargo, especially delivery of cargo without demanding the production of an original bill of lading. These claims are not covered.

c. MEMBERSHIP TO P&I CLUBS

i. Membership Conditions

The owner who wants the vessel to be protected under P&I insurance, makes a contract with a P&I Club which is called "policy" and becomes a member of that Club. The owner should give all details concerning the vessel to the Club. These details given by the owner will be accepted as the base of the insurance contract. In case of misinformation, if the owner is not accepted yet, it will not be accepted or if it is accepted, the loss will not be covered by the Club. The management of the Club can refuse the membership of an owner without giving a reason. Once the surveys are completed by the Club, "Certificate of Entry" is given to the owner.

Unless otherwise provided by the rules of the Club, the insurance period begins from the date and hour, which are mentioned on the certificate of entry and unless the insurance is cancelled, continues to the 20th February of the next policy year.

During the insurance period, the owners shall pay the premiums in order to create the "pool" from which the possible loss should be covered. The owners shall pay advance call, which is the premium that is paid at the beginning of every policy year. Or the Club may need supplementary calls determined by the board of directors or additional calls in case of a casualty. Finally we have releance calls which are paid by the owners who is leaving the Club as it shall not pay premiums anymore.

ii. Termination of Membership

The conditions terminating the membership are determined in a detailed way within the Club rules.

- Termination notice by the Club
- Death or bankruptcy of the member or if he could not govern the vessel or of it is a company, end of the company

- Nonpayment of premiums
- If the vessel is mortgaged
- Modification of head of the company
- Confiscation of the vessel
- Total loss of the vessel etc.

- 37 -

d. CONCLUSION

P&I insurance, being one of the three important marine insurance types, covers the ship owner's legal liabilities towards third parties, who may have a legal or contractual claim against the vessel. It is important to bear in mind that the P&I Club never assumes the owner's liability, therefore technically the ship owner who is a member of the P&I Club as well, is always responsible for payments. In practice the P&I Club takes over the business of handling the claims and ensuring that payments are correctly made.

BIBLIOGRAPHY

BOOKS:

CARR, Indira – STONE, Peter, **International Trade Law**, Routledge, Fifth Edition, Oxon, 2014, 792 p.

CARR, Indira – STONE, Peter, **International Trade Law**, Routledge – Cavendish, Fourth Edition, Oxon, 2010, 738 p.

DOCKRAY, Martin, **Cases & Materials on the Carriage of Goods by Sea**, Cavendish Publishing, Third Edition, 2003, 512 p.

LAWES, Edward, **A Practical Treatise on Charter parties of Affreightment, Bills of Lading, and Stoppage in Transitu, With an Appendix of Precedents**, Printed by S. Brooke, 35, Paternoster-Row and Sold by Messrs. Butterworth and Son, Fleet Street; Clarke and Sons, Portugal Street; R. Pheney, Inner Temple Lane; and S. Sweet, Chancery Lane London, 1813, 603 p.

PARSONS, Theophilus, **A Treatise on Maritime Law, including the Law of Shipping; the Law of Marine Insurance; and the Law and Practice of Admiralty**, Little Brown and Company, Boston, 1859, 780 p.

WILSON, John F., **Carriage of Goods by Sea**, Pierson – Longman, Sixth Edition, Southampton, 2008, 523 p.

ARTICLES:

BAXI, Upendra, "Unification of Private Maritime International Law through Treaties – An Assessment", **Indian Year Book of International Affairs**, 1965, pp. 72-163.
http://upendrabaxi.net/documents/Unification%20of%20private%20martime%20international%20law%20through%20treatie.pdf (27.04.2014)

GAUCI, Gotthard, "Limitation of Liability in Maritime Law, an anachronism?", **Marine Policy**, Vol. 19, No. 1, 1995, pp. 65-74.

http://202.114.89.60/resource/pdf/1847.pdf (27.04.2014)

HARE, John, Limitation of Liability in Shipping, **University of Cape Town,** Nigeria, 2004, 20 p.

http://web.uct.ac.za/depts/shiplaw/fulltext/harepapers/limliab-nigeria.pdf (27.04.2014)

KEENAN, Roman T., "Charter Parties and Bills of Lading", **Marquette Law Review,** Vol. 42, Milwaukee, 1959, pp. 346-361.

http://scholarship.law.marquette.edu/cgi/viewcontent.cgi?article=2917&context=mulr (27.04.2014)

REYNOLDS, Francis, "The Hague Rules, the Hague-Visby Rules, and the Hamburg Rules", **the MLAANZ New Wealand Branch Conference,** Tokaanu, 1990.

http://www.fd.unl.pt/docentes_docs/ma/wks_MA_20178.pdf (27.04.2014)

YIANNOPOULAS, Athanassios N., "Conflict Problems in International Bills of Lading: Validity of Negligence Clauses", **Louisiana Law Review,** Vol. 18, No. 4, June 1958.

http://digitalcommons.law.lsu.edu/cgi/viewcontent.cgi?article=2609&context=lalrev (27.04.2014)

CASE LAW:

Boucher v. Lawson, Cas. T. hard 53 ; 95 E. R. 116.

http://unisetca.ipower.com/other/css/95ER53.html (27.04.2014)

Sea & Land Securities Ltd v. William Dickinson & Co Ltd, 2 KB 65, 1942.

http://law.ato.gov.au/atolaw/view.htm?rank=find&criteria=AND~Bills~basic~exact&target=E%20EA&style=html&sdocid=TXR/TR20032/NAT/ATO/00001&recStart=21&PiT=99991231235958&recnum=35&tot=72&pn=ALL:::EA (27.04.2014)

Mississippi Shipping Co v. Zander and Company, 270 F.2d 345, 5th Cir. 1959, United States Court of Appeal.

https://casetext.com/case/mississippi-shipping-co-v-zander-and-company#.U17El_1_uSo (27.04.2014)

Sommaire

I. CHARTERER'S RISKS AND LIABILITIES .... - 7 -

   a. INTRODUCTION .... - 7 -

      i. Charterparty .... - 7 -

      ii. Charterer .... - 7 -

      iii. Carrier .... - 7 -

   b. TYPES OF CHARTERER .... - 7 -

      i. Demise or Bareboat Charterers .... - 7 -

      ii. Time Charterers .... - 8 -

      iii. Voyage Charterers .... - 8 -

   c. RISING OF RISKS AND LIABILITIES OF CHARTERER .... - 8 -

      i. By Contract .... - 8 -

      ii. In Tort or Delict .... - 9 -

      iii. Statutory Liability .... - 9 -

   d. COMMON SITUATIONS WHERE A CHARTERER MAY FACE
LIABILITY .... - 9 -

      i. Loss of or Damage to Cargo .... - 9 -

      ii. Personal Injury .... - 10 -

      iii. Pollution .... - 10 -

      iv. Damage to Hull .... - 10 -

      v. Fines .... - 11 -

      vi. General Average, Salvage and Special Charges .... - 11 -

      vii. Legal Costs and Related Expenses .... - 11 -

   e. CONCLUSION .... - 12 -

II. NEGLIGENCE CLAUSE IN CHARTERPARTY .... - 13 -

   a. INTRODUCTION .... - 13 -

      i. General .... - 13 -

      iv. Contract of affreightment and charterparty .... - 15 -

   b. EVOLUTION OF NEGLIGENCE CLAUSES IN LIGHT OF "LIMITATION
OF LIABILITY" CONCEPT .... - 18 -

i. Historical background ....- 18 -

ii. Place of negligence clauses on the international scene ....- 19 -

c. NEGLIGENCE CLAUSES IN FIVE STEPS ....- 21 -

i. Who ....- 21 -

ii. To whom ....- 22 -

iii. What ....- 23 -

iv. When ....- 23 -

v. Where ....- 24 -

d. NEGLIGENCE CLAUSES REGULATIONS ....- 24 -

i. Hague Rules ....- 24 -

ii. Hague-Visby Rules ....- 25 -

iii. Hamburg Rules ....- 25 -

e. VALIDITY OF NEGLIGENCE CLAUSES ....- 26 -

i. England ....- 27 -

ii. United States ....- 28 -

iii. France ....- 30 -

f. CONCLUSION ....- 31 -

III. PROTECTION AND INDEMNITY INSURANCE ....- 33 -

a. INTRODUCTION ....- 33 -

i. Key Notions ....- 33 -

ii. History ....- 34 -

b. ROLE OF P&I CLUBS ....- 34 -

i. Service ....- 34 -

ii. Cover ....- 35 -

c. MEMBERSHIP TO P&I CLUBS ....- 36 -

i. Membership Conditions ....- 36 -

ii. Termination of Membership ....- 36 -

d. CONCLUSION ....- 37 -

BIBLIOGRAPHY ....- 38 -